HAL•LEONARD®
GUITAR PLAY-ALONG

AUDIO ACCESS INCLUDED

VOL. 84

STEELY DAN

Photo: © John Atashian / Retna Ltd.

Tracking, mixing, and mastering by
Jake Johnson & Bill Maynard at Paradyme Productions
All guitars by Doug Boduch
Bass by Tom McGirr
Keyboards by Warren Wiegratz
Drums by Scott Schroedl

PLAYBACK+
Speed • Pitch • Balance • Loop

To access audio, visit:
www.halleonard.com/mylibrary

Enter Code
3989-8412-0307-4563

ISBN 978-1-4234-3209-8

HAL•LEONARD®

Visit Hal Leonard Online at
www.halleonard.com

Contact us:
Hal Leonard
7777 West Bluemound Road
Milwaukee, WI 53213
Email: info@halleonard.com

In Europe, contact:
Hal Leonard Europe Limited
42 Wigmore Street
Marylebone, London, W1U 2RN
Email: info@halleonardeurope.com

In Australia, contact:
Hal Leonard Australia Pty. Ltd.
4 Lentara Court
Cheltenham, Victoria, 3192 Australia
Email: info@halleonard.com.au

Guitar Notation Legend

THE MUSICAL STAFF shows pitches and rhythms and is divided by bar lines into measures. Pitches are named after the first seven letters of the alphabet.

TABLATURE graphically represents the guitar fingerboard. Each horizontal line represents a string, and each number represents a fret.

4th string, 2nd fret   1st & 2nd strings open, played together   open D chord

HALF-STEP BEND: Strike the note and bend up 1/2 step.

WHOLE-STEP BEND: Strike the note and bend up one step.

GRACE NOTE BEND: Strike the note and immediately bend up as indicated.

SLIGHT (MICROTONE) BEND: Strike the note and bend up 1/4 step.

BEND AND RELEASE: Strike the note and bend up as indicated, then release back to the original note. Only the first note is struck.

PRE-BEND: Bend the note as indicated, then strike it.

VIBRATO: The string is vibrated by rapidly bending and releasing the note with the fretting hand.

PALM MUTING: The note is partially muted by the pick hand lightly touching the string(s) just before the bridge.

HAMMER-ON: Strike the first (lower) note with one finger, then sound the higher note (on the same string) with another finger by fretting it without picking.

PULL-OFF: Place both fingers on the notes to be sounded. Strike the first note and without picking, pull the finger off to sound the second (lower) note.

LEGATO SLIDE: Strike the first note and then slide the same fret-hand finger up or down to the second note. The second note is not struck.

SHIFT SLIDE: Same as legato slide, except the second note is struck.

TRILL: Very rapidly alternate between the notes indicated by continuously hammering on and pulling off.

TAPPING: Hammer ("tap") the fret indicated with the pick-hand index or middle finger and pull off to the note fretted by the fret hand.

NATURAL HARMONIC: Strike the note while the fret-hand lightly touches the string directly over the fret indicated.

PINCH HARMONIC: The note is fretted normally and a harmonic is produced by adding the edge of the thumb or the tip of the index finger of the pick hand to the normal pick attack.

TREMOLO PICKING: The note is picked as rapidly and continuously as possible.

VIBRATO BAR DIVE AND RETURN: The pitch of the note or chord is dropped a specified number of steps (in rhythm), then returned to the original pitch.

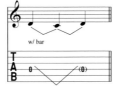

VIBRATO BAR SCOOP: Depress the bar just before striking the note, then quickly release the bar.

VIBRATO BAR DIP: Strike the note and then immediately drop a specified number of steps, then release back to the original pitch.

Additional Musical Definitions

 *(accent)* • Accentuate note (play it louder).

 (staccato) • Play the note short.

D.S. al Coda • Go back to the sign (%), then play until the measure marked "*To Coda*," then skip to the section labelled "**Coda**."

D.C. al Fine • Go back to the beginning of the song and play until the measure marked "*Fine*" (end).

Fill • Label used to identify a brief melodic figure which is to be inserted into the arrangement.

N.C. • Harmony is implied.

 • Repeat measures between signs.

 • When a repeated section has different endings, play the first ending only the first time and the second ending only the second time.

HAL•LEONARD®

GUITAR
PLAY-ALONG

AUDIO
ACCESS
INCLUDED

STEELY DAN

CONTENTS

Page	Title
4	FM
12	Hey Nineteen
28	Josie
34	Kid Charlemagne
19	My Old School
40	Peg
47	Pretzel Logic
54	Reeling in the Years

FM

from the film FM
Words and Music by Walter Becker and Donald Fagen

Intro
Moderately ♩ = 110

w/ clean tone

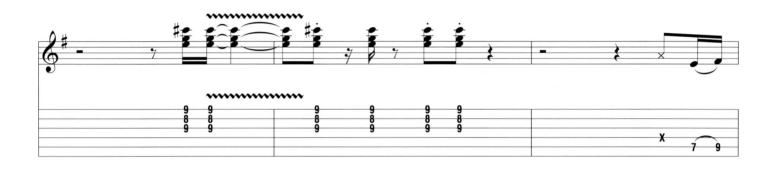

Verse

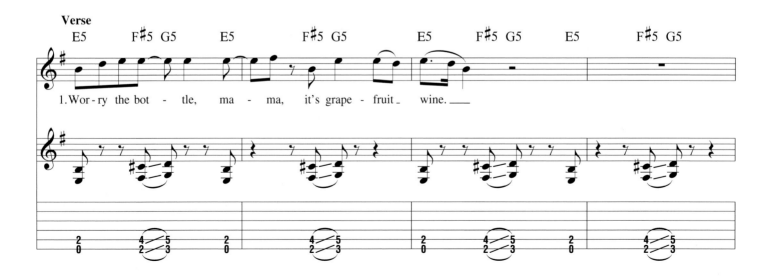

1. Wor-ry the bot - tle, ma - ma, it's grape-fruit_ wine. ___

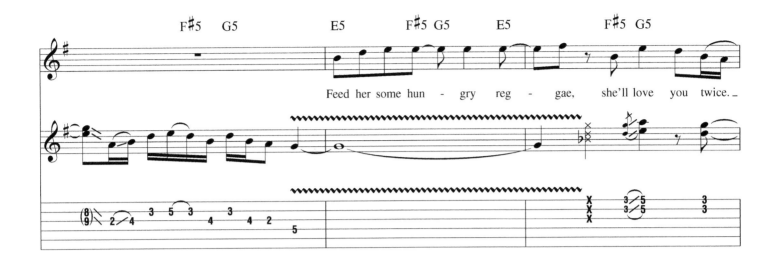

Feed her some hun - gry reg - gae, she'll love you twice.

— The girls __ don't seem to care __ to - night, __ as

dist. off

long as __ the mood is right. __ No stat - ic at all. __

Gtr. tacet

__ F - M. No stat - ic at all. __

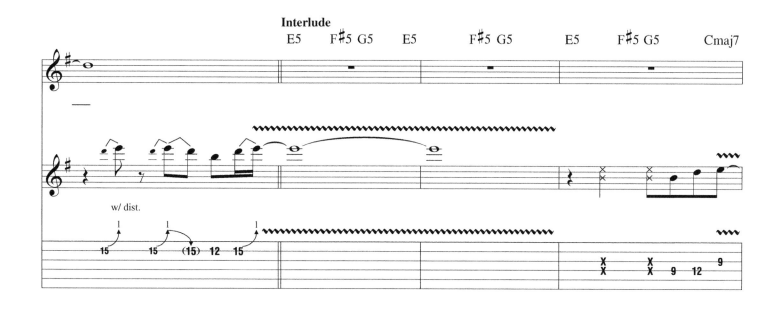

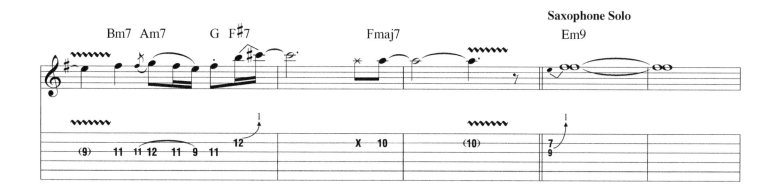

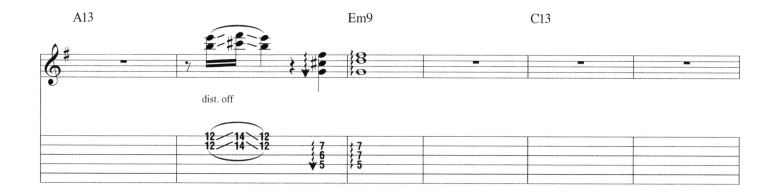

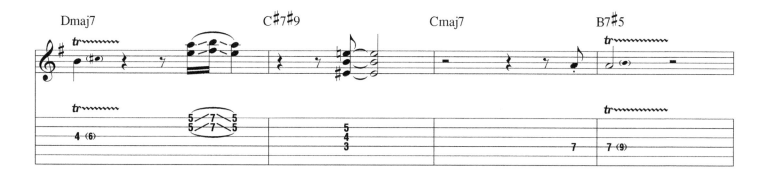

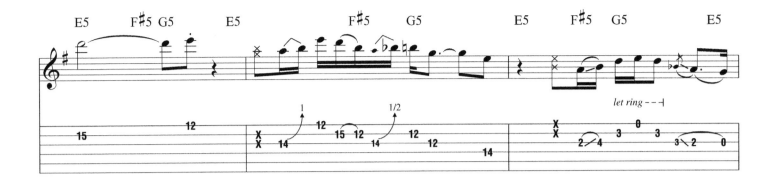

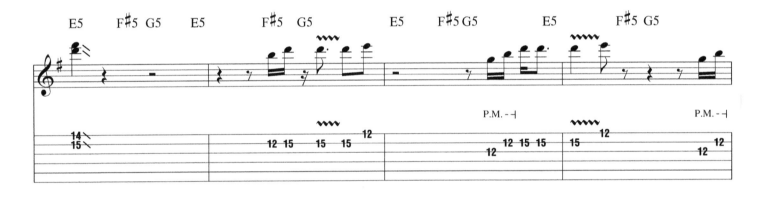

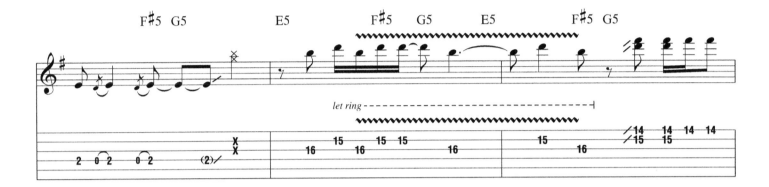

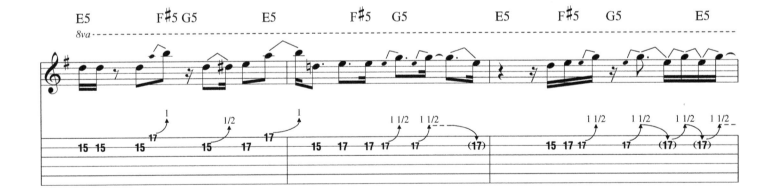

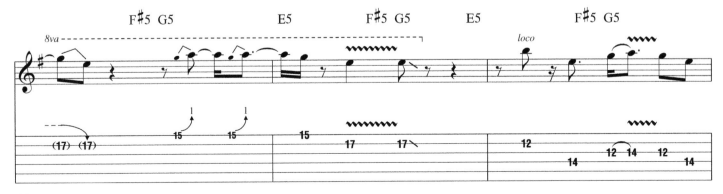

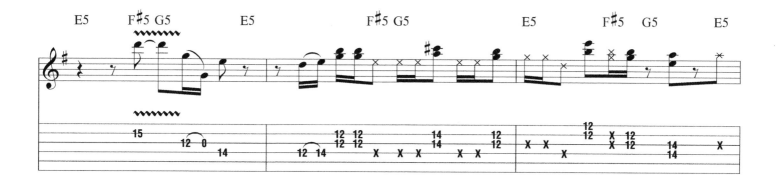

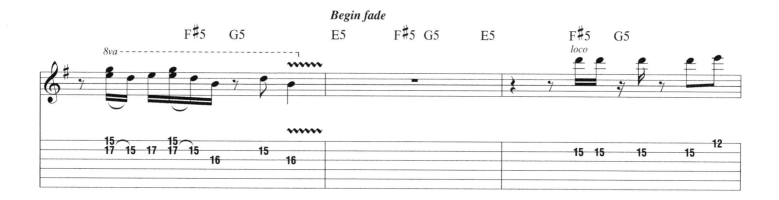

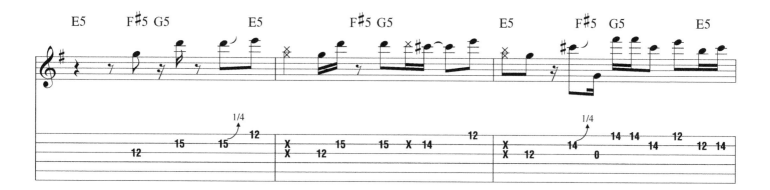

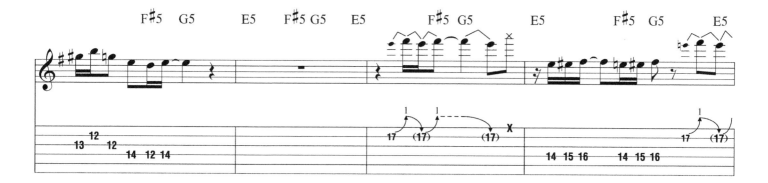

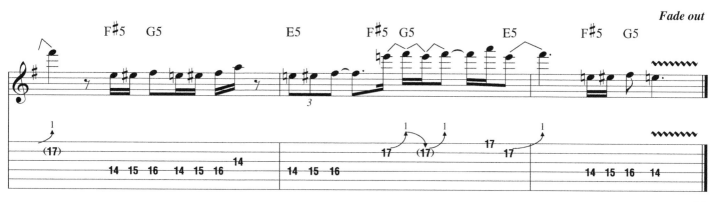

Hey Nineteen

Words and Music by Walter Becker and Donald Fagen

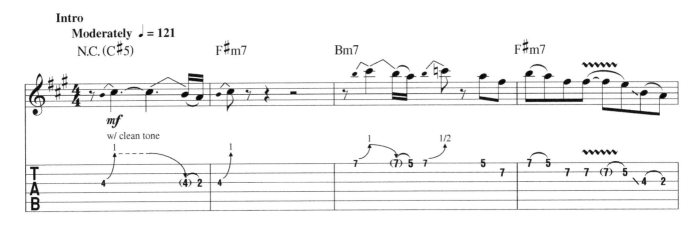

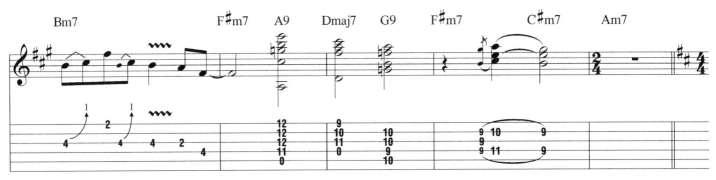

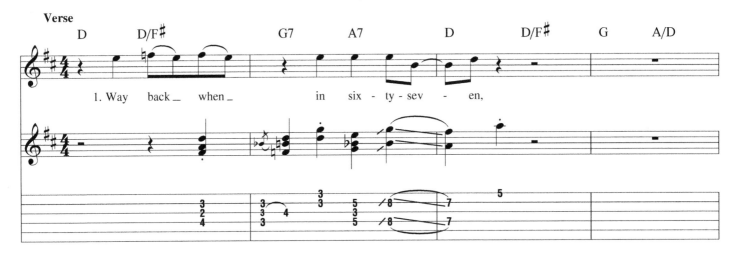

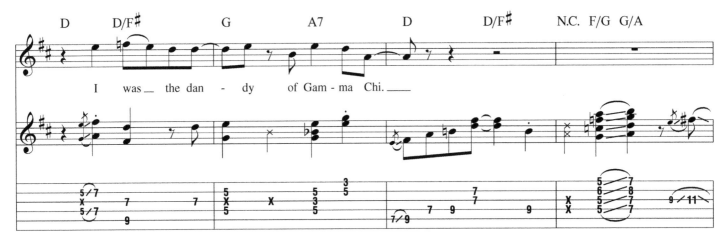

⊕ Coda

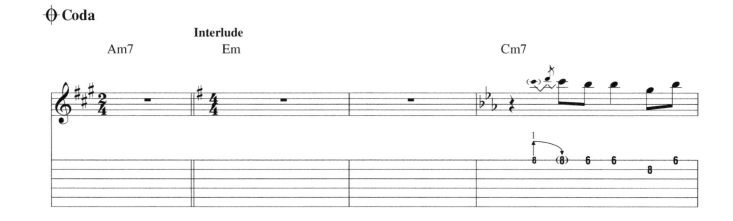

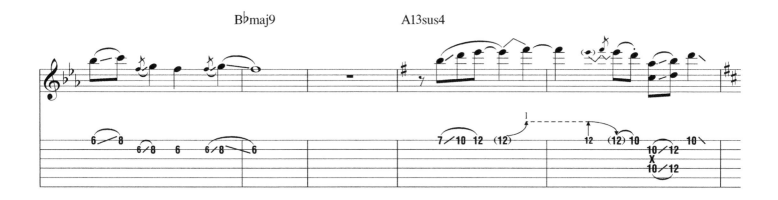

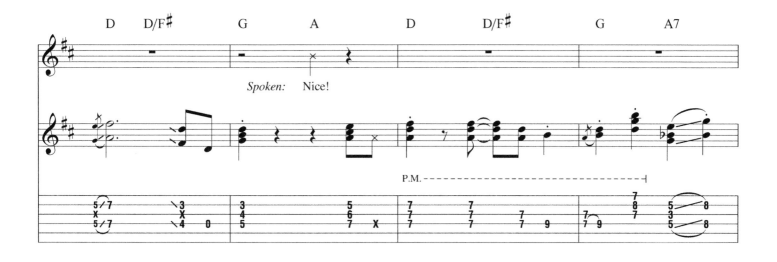

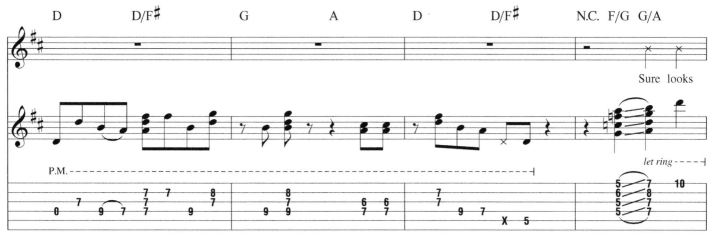

15

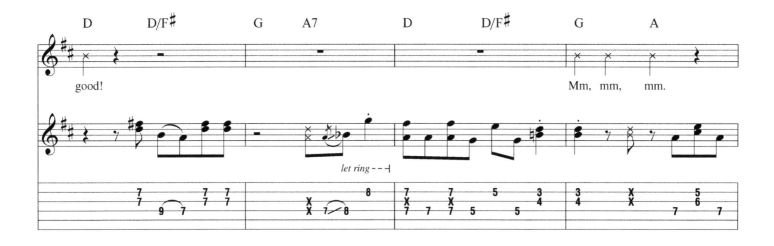

Bridge

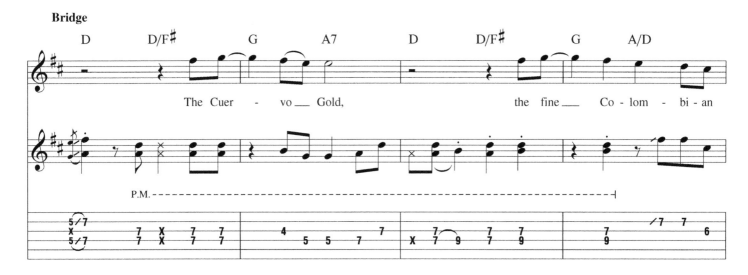

Chorus

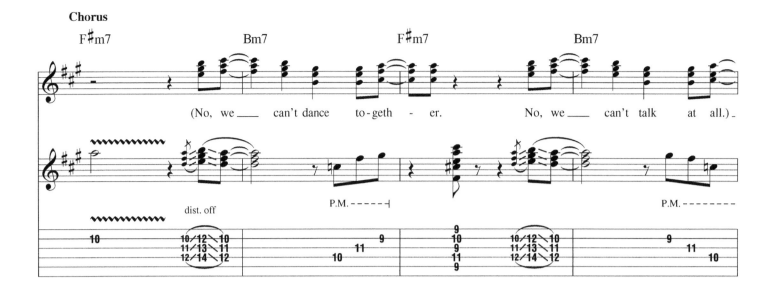

(No, we ___ can't dance to-geth - er. No, we ___ can't talk at all.)

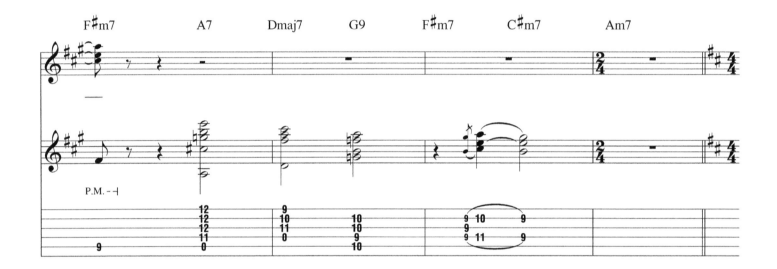

Outro

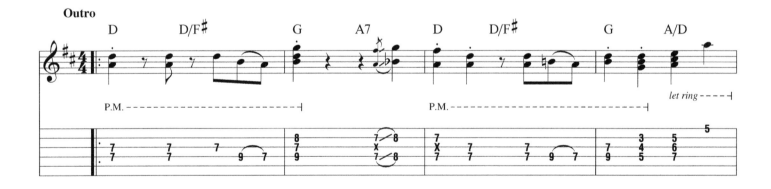

Repeat and fade

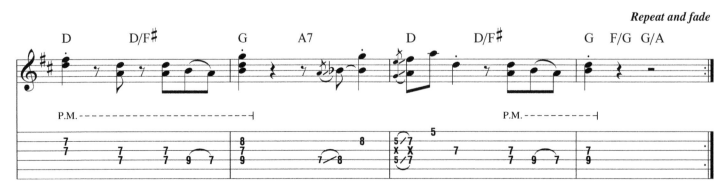

My Old School

Words and Music by Walter Becker and Donald Fagen

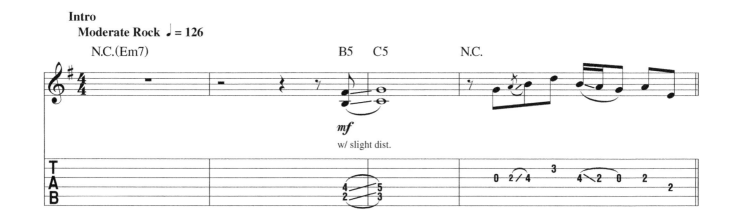

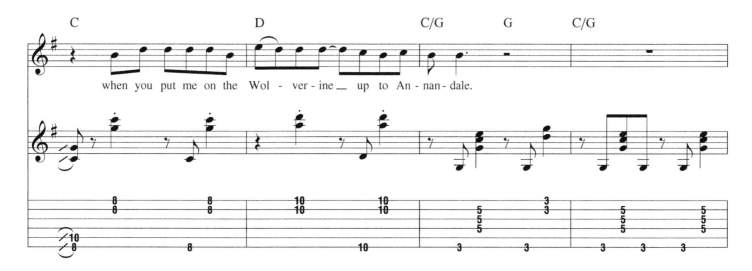

It was still Sep-tem - ber ___ when your dad-dy was quite sur-prised ___

to find you with the work - ing girls ___ in the coun - ty jail. I was

smok - in' with the boys up - stairs ___ when I heard a - bout the whole af - fair, ___ I said,

whoa, no, ___ Wil - liam and Mar - y won't do, now. ___

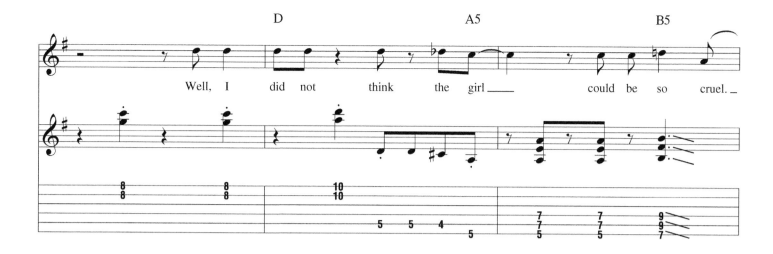

Well, I did not think the girl ___ could be so cruel. ___

And I'm nev-er go-in' back ___

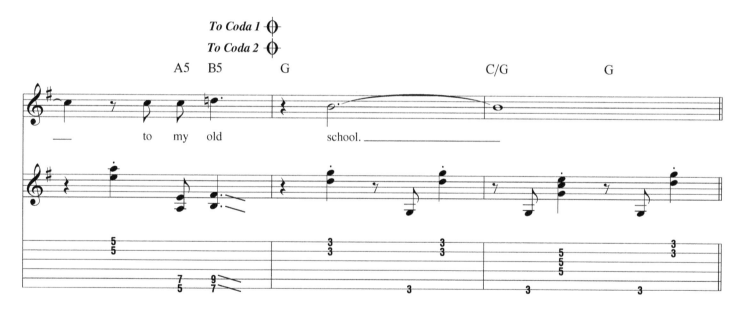

___ to my old school. ___

Guitar Solo

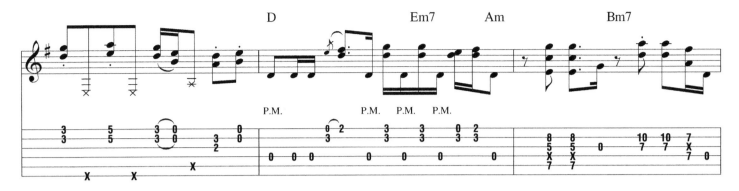

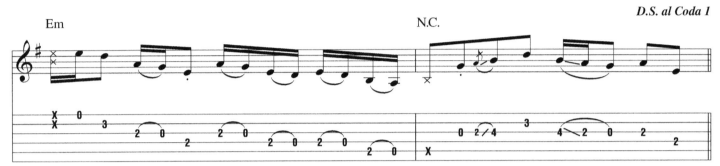

D.S. al Coda 1

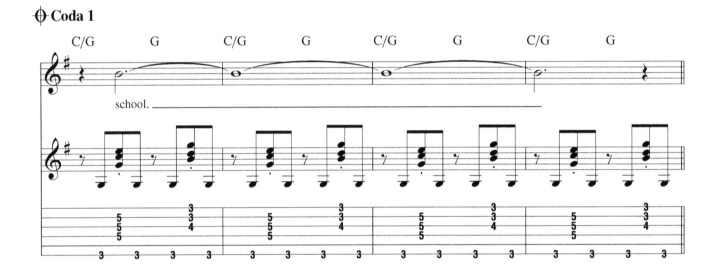

Coda 1

Guitar Solo

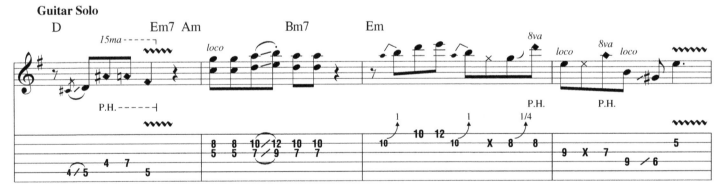

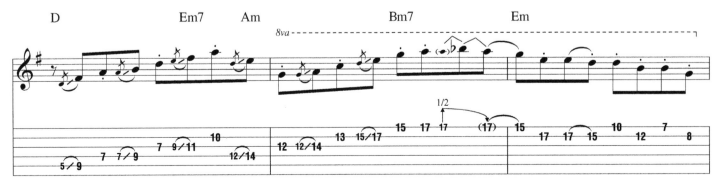

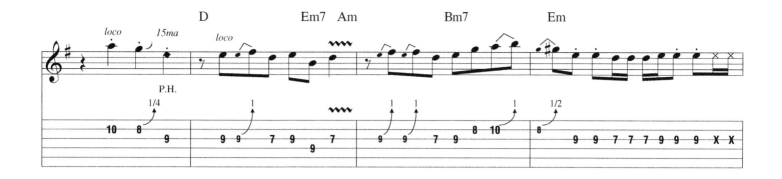

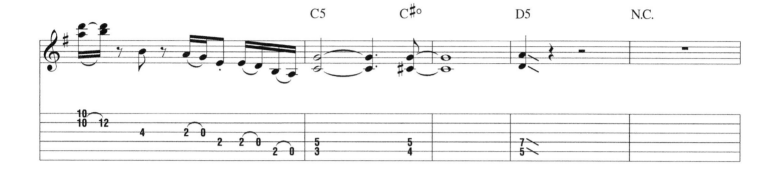

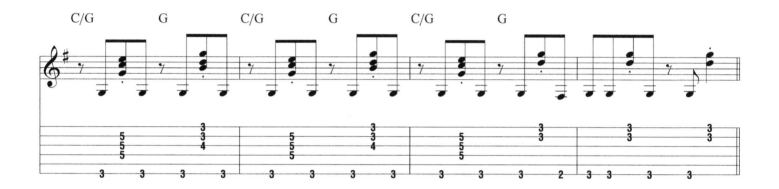

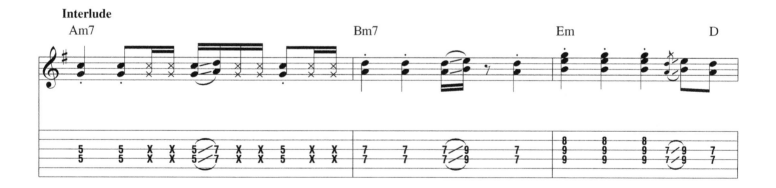

Interlude

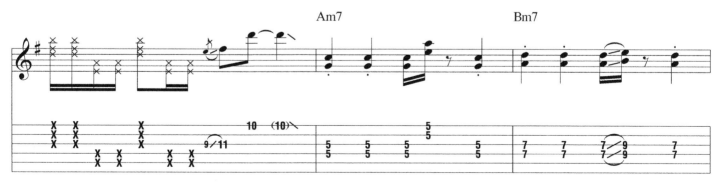

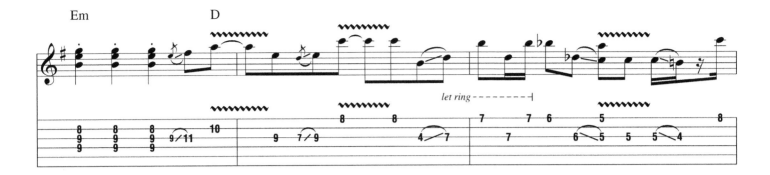

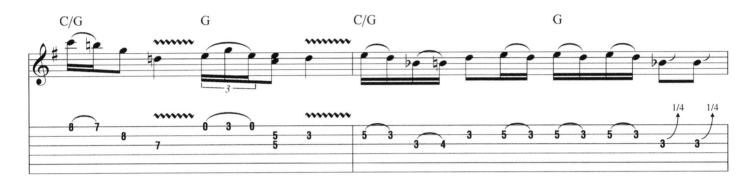

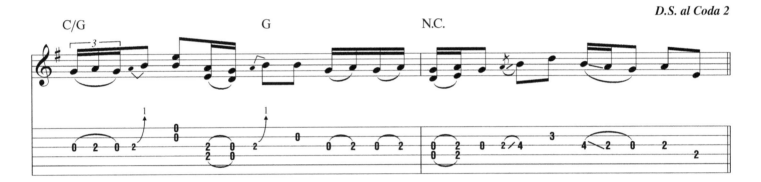

D.S. al Coda 2

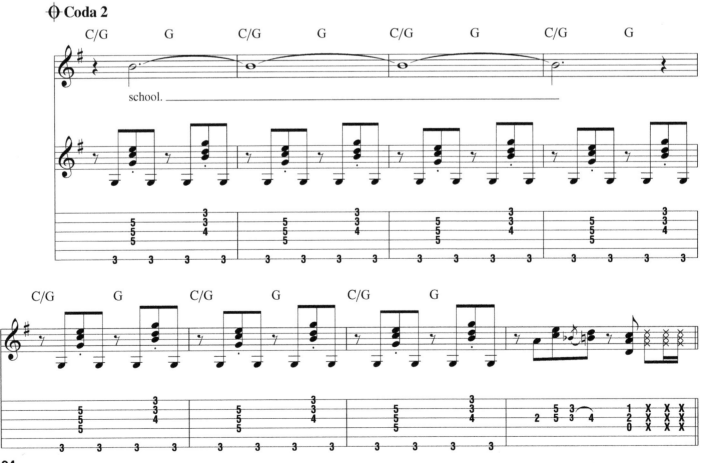

Outro-Guitar Solo

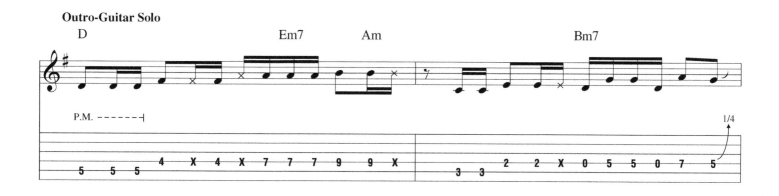

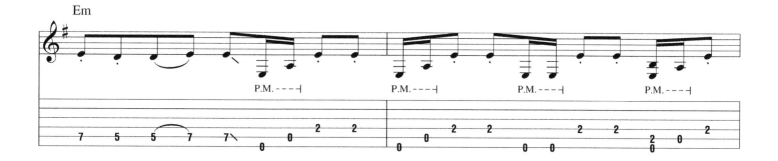

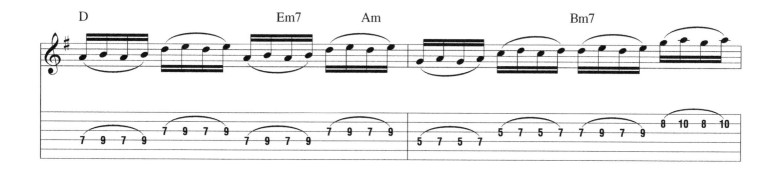

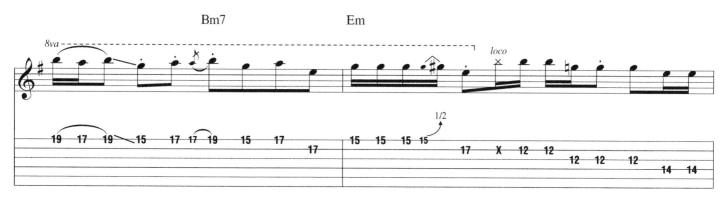

25

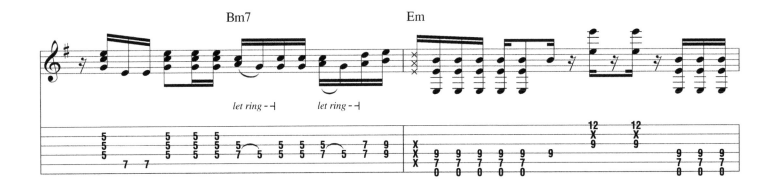

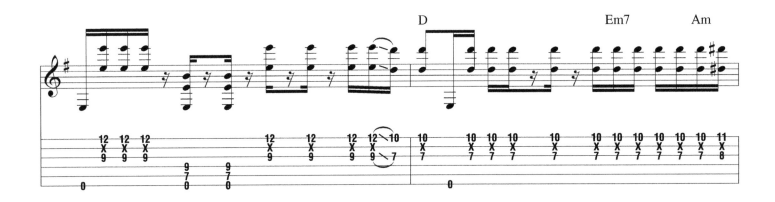

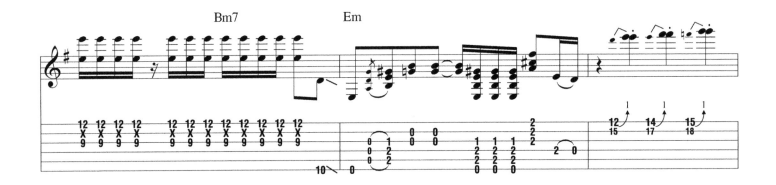

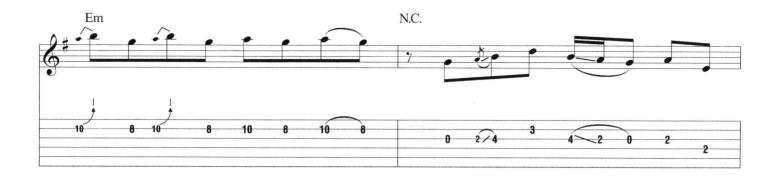

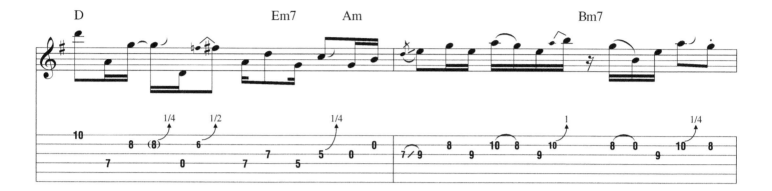

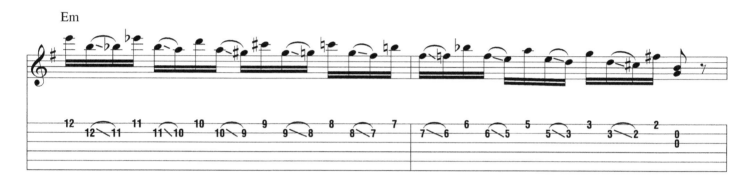

Fade out

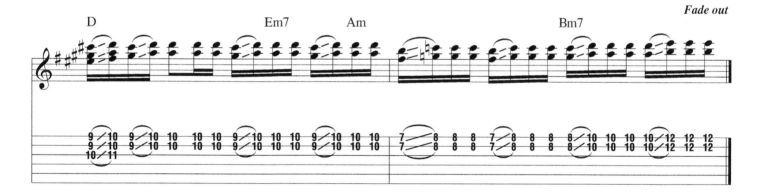

Additional Lyrics

2. Oleanders growin' outside her door. Soon they're gonna be in bloom up in Annandale.
I can't stand her doin' what she did before, livin' like a gypsy queen in a fairy tale.
Well, I hear the whistle but I can't go, I'm gonna take her down to Mexico.
She said a, "Whoa, no, Guadalajara won't do, now."
Well, I did not think the girl could be so cruel. And I'm never goin' back to my old school.

3. California tumbles into the sea; that'll be the day I go back to Annandale.
Tried to warn you about Gino and Daddy G, but I can't seem to get to you through the U.S. mail.
Well, I hear the whistle but I can't go, I'm gonna take her down to Mexico.
She said a, "Whoa, no, Guadalajara won't do, now."
Well, I did not think the girl could be so cruel. And I'm never goin' back to my old school.

Josie

Words and Music by Walter Becker and Donald Fagen

Intro
Moderate Jazz Rock ♩ = 121

N.C.

C/F   F#7#9   D/G   A♭maj7   Em7

Play 7 times

Verse
Em7

1. We're gon-na   break out the hats __ and hoo-ters   when Jo-sie comes

2. *See additional lyrics*

home. __   We're gon-na   rev up the mo-tor scoot-

-ers when Jo - sie comes home __ to stay, __ we're gon - na park in the street.

Sleep on the beach __ and make __ it. Throw down the jam 'til the

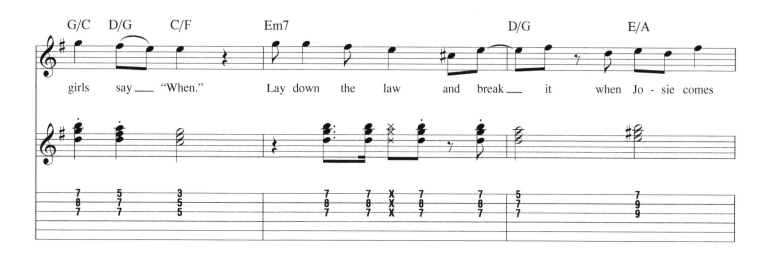

girls say __ "When." Lay down the law and break __ it when Jo - sie comes

home. __ When Jo - sie comes home, so good. __

See additional lyrics

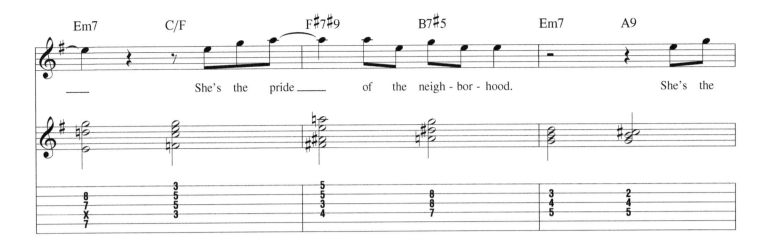

She's the pride ___ of the neigh-bor-hood. She's the

To Coda ⊕

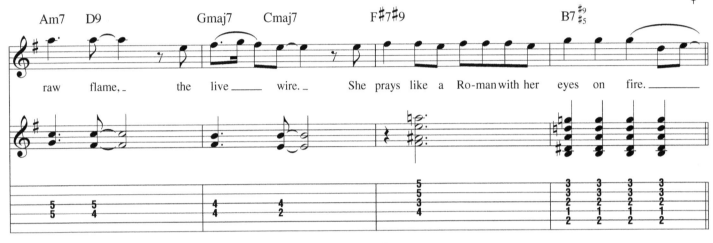

raw flame, ___ the live ___ wire. ___ She prays like a Ro-man with her eyes on fire. ___

1.

Interlude

2.

Bridge

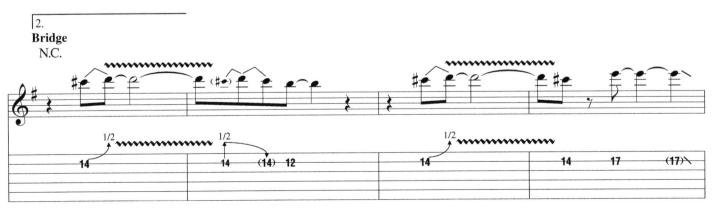

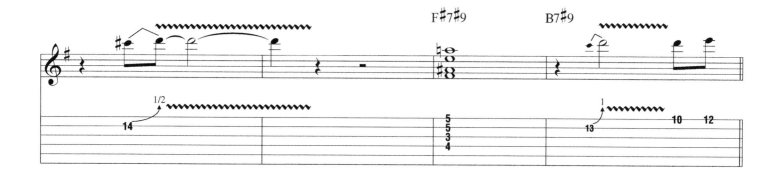

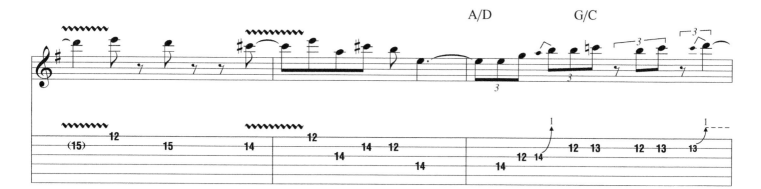

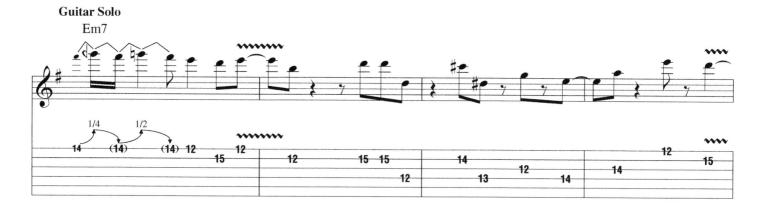

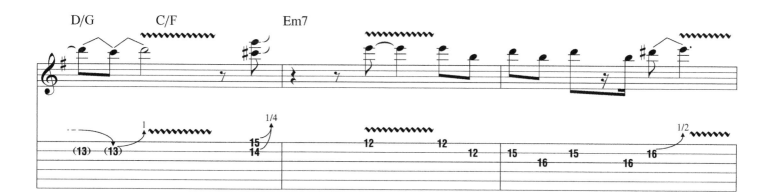

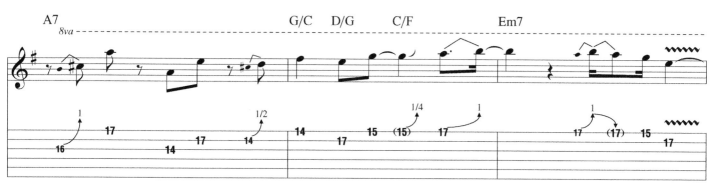

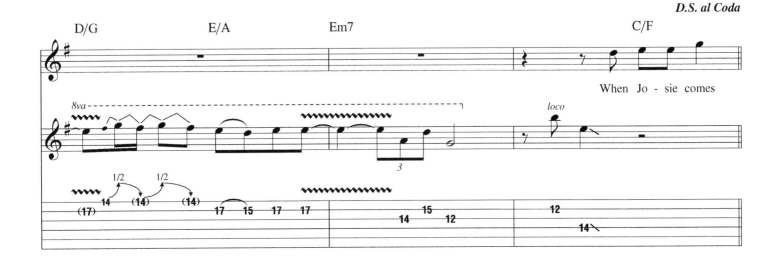

When Jo - sie comes

Coda

Outro

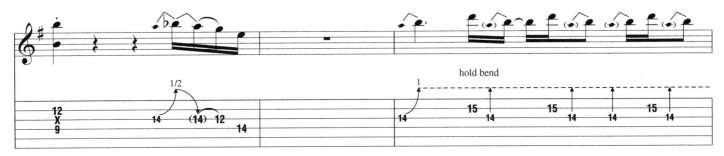

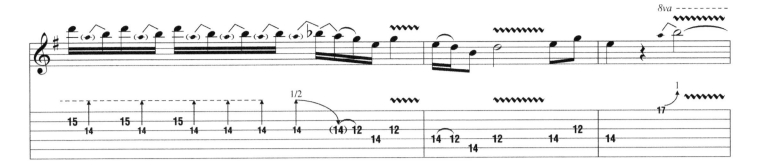

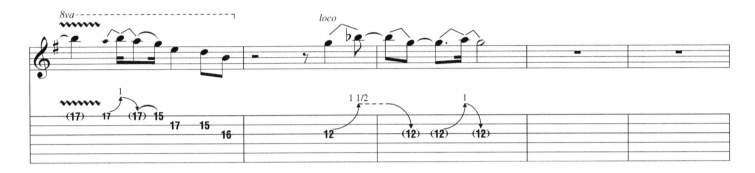

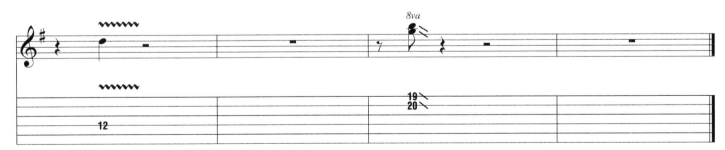

Additional Lyrics

2. Jo, would you love to scrapple? She'll never say "No." No.
   Shine up the battle apple, we'll shake 'em all down tonight, we're gonna mix in the street.
   Strike at the stroke of midnight. Dance on the bones 'til the girls say "When."
   Pick up what's left by daylight when Josie comes home.

Chorus When Josie comes home, so bad. She's the best friend we never had.
   She's the raw flame, the live wire. She prays like a Roman with her eyes on fire.

Kid Charlemagne

Words and Music by Walter Becker and Donald Fagen

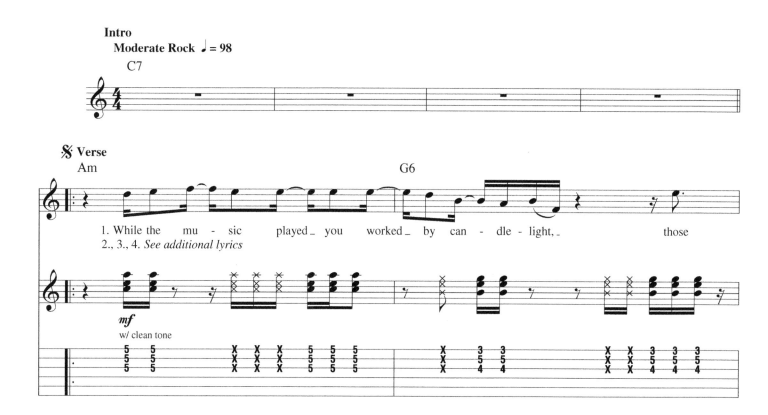

turned it on ___ the world, ___ that's when you turned ___ the world ___ a - round. ___

Did you feel _____ like Je - sus? Did you re - al - ize ___

___ that you were a cham - pion in their eyes? _____

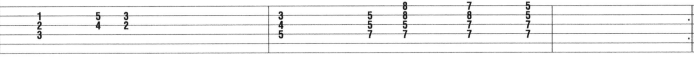

Chorus

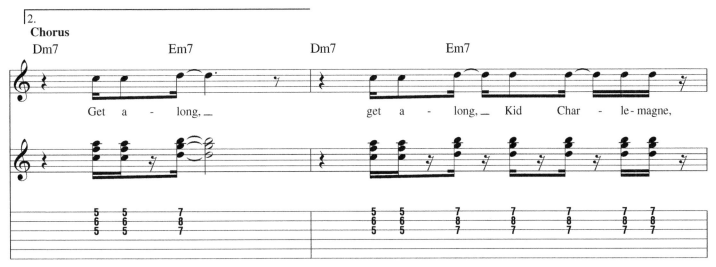

Get a - long, ___ get a - long, ___ Kid Char - le - magne,

get a - long __ Kid Char - le - magne. __

1st time, D.S. (take 2nd ending)

2nd time, To Coda 1

3rd time, To Coda 2

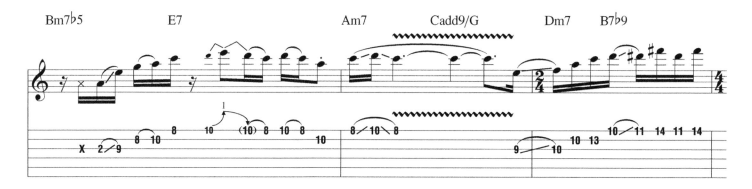

Coda 1

Guitar Solo

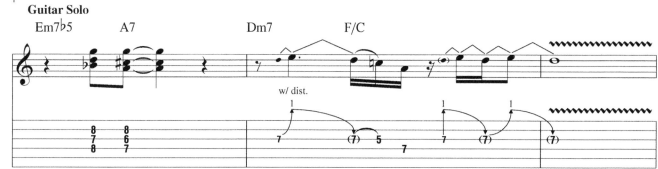

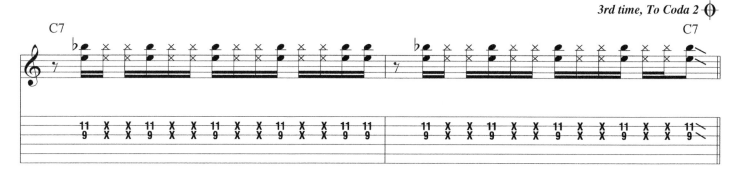

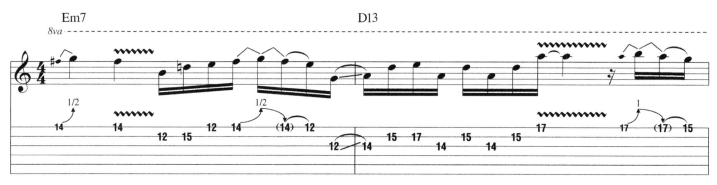

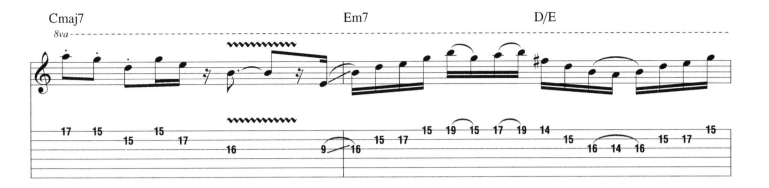

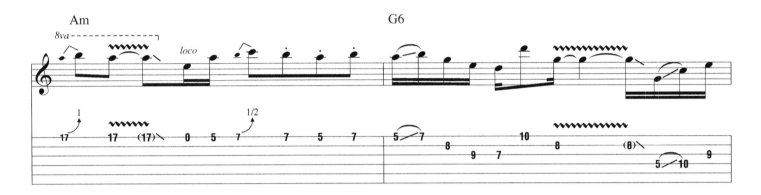

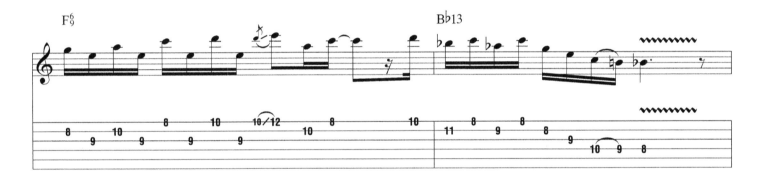

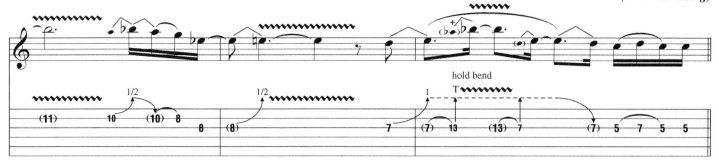

⊕ Coda 2

Outro-Guitar Solo

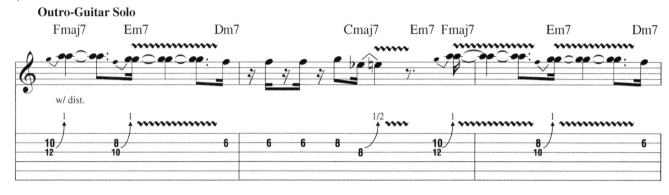

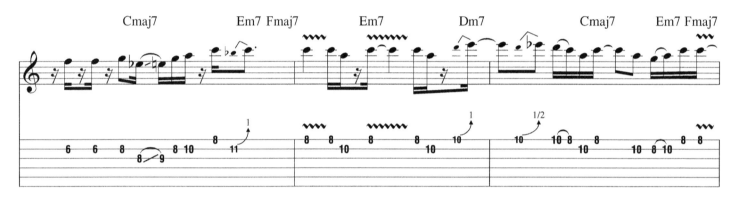

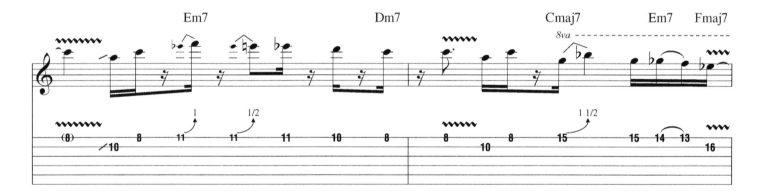

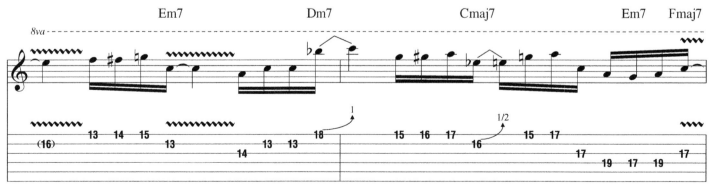

Additional Lyrics

2. On the hill the stuff was laced with kerosene, but yours was kitchen-clean.
   Ev'ryone stopped to stare at your technicolor motorhome.
   Ev'ry A-frame had your number on the wall, you must've had it all,
   You'd go to L.A. on a dare, and you'd go it alone.
   Could you last forever? Could you see the day,
   Could you feel your whole world fall apart and fade away?

3. Now your patrons have all left you in the red,
   Your low-rent friends are dead, this life can be very strange.
   All those day-glo freaks who used to paint the face,
   They've joined the human race. Some things will never change.
   Son, you are mistaken. You are obsolete,
   Look at all the white men on the street.

4. Clean this mess up else we'll all end up in jail,
   Those test tubes and the scale, just get it all out of here.
   Is there gas in the car? Yes, there's gas in the car.
   I think the people down the hall know who you are.
   Careful what you carry, 'cause the man is wise.
   You are still an outlaw in their eyes.

Peg

Words and Music by Walter Becker and Donald Fagen

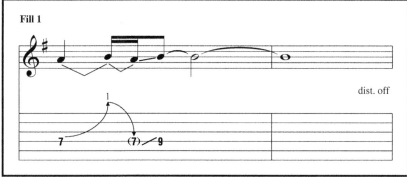

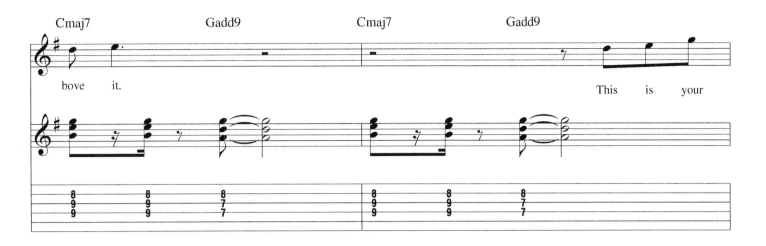

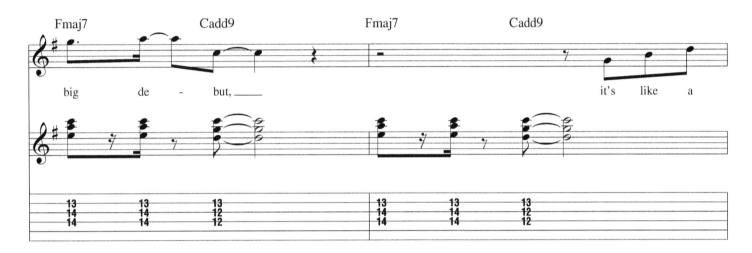

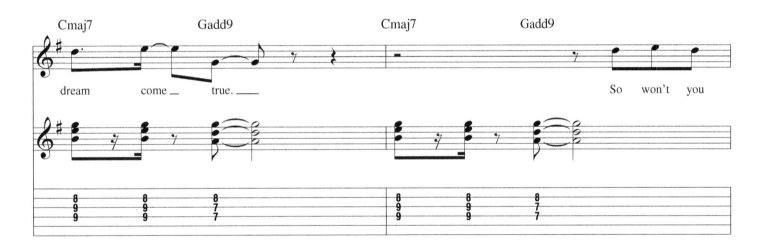

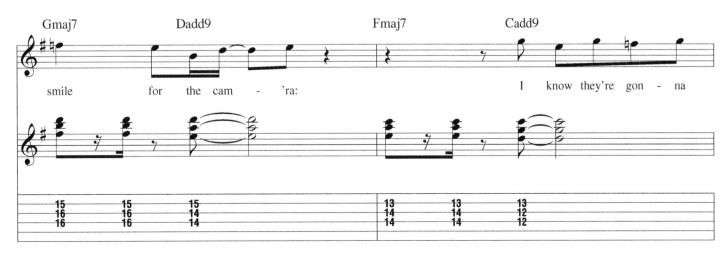

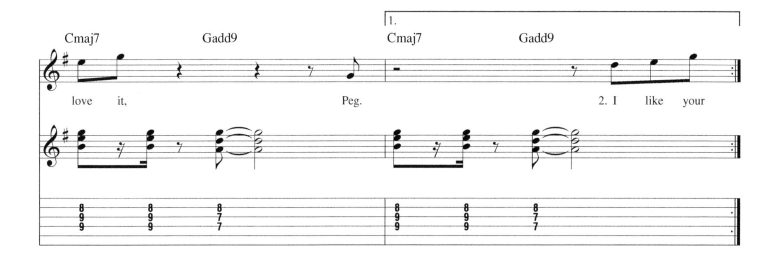

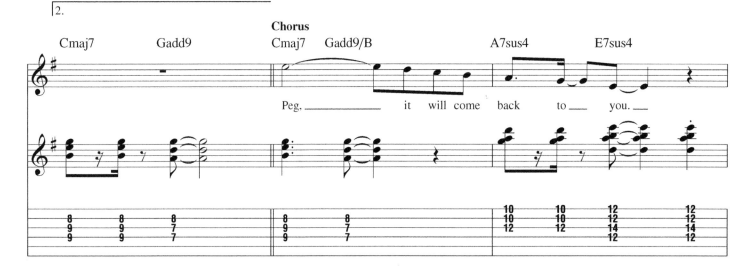

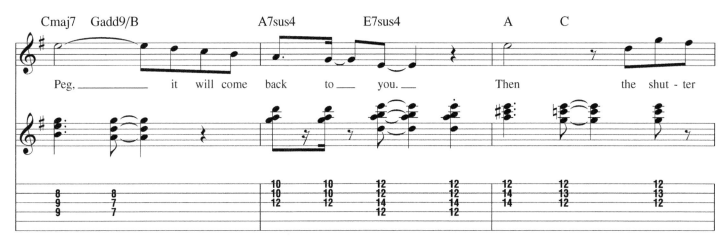

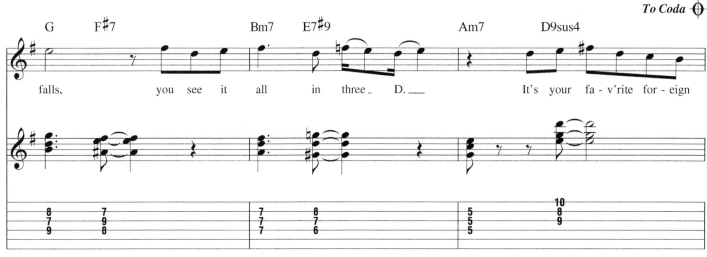

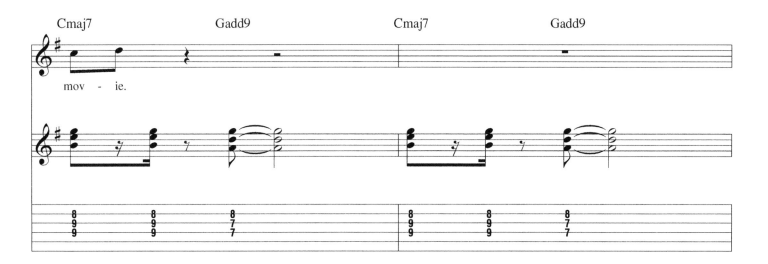

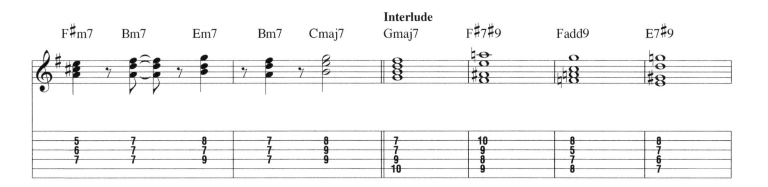

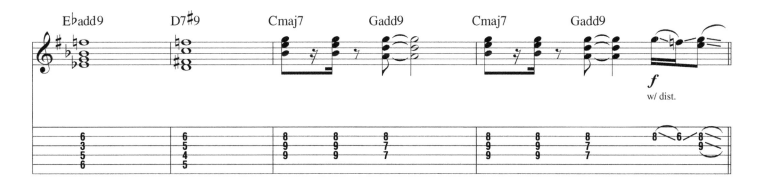

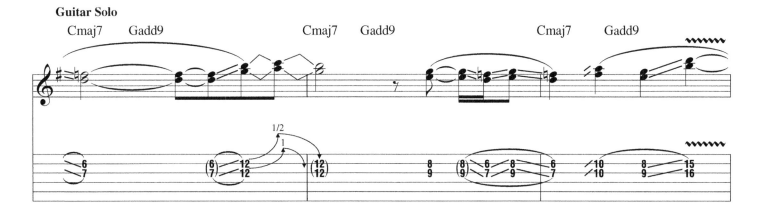

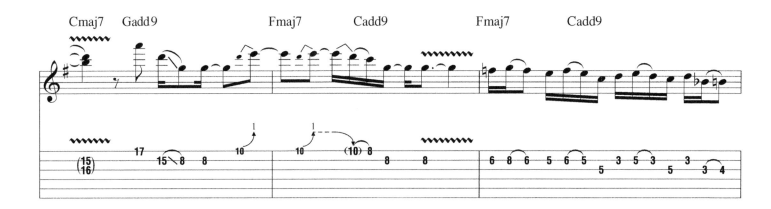

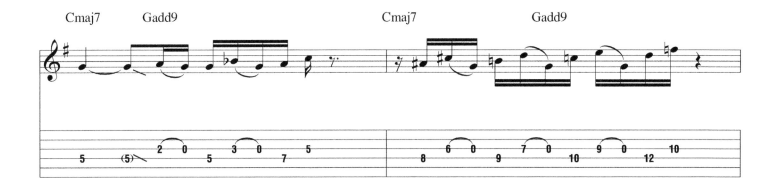

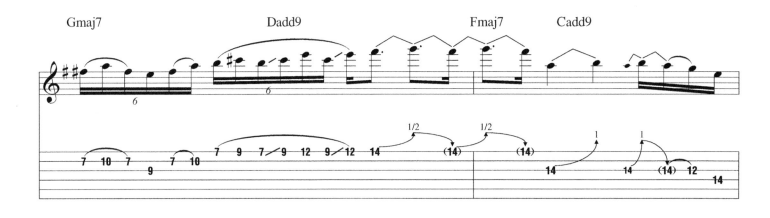

D.S. al Coda
(take 2nd ending)

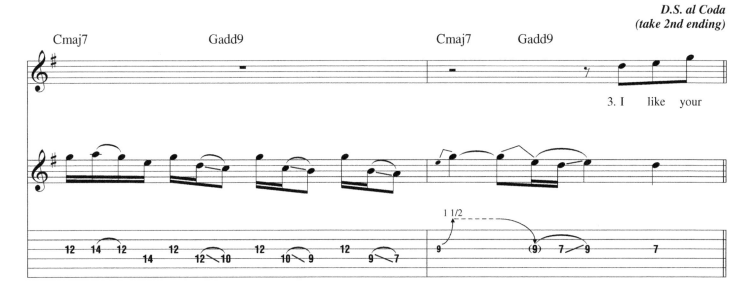

3. I   like   your

Coda

Outro

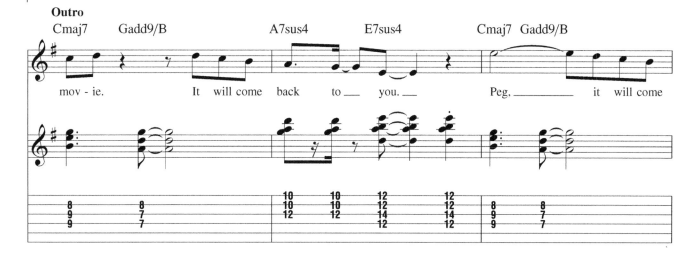

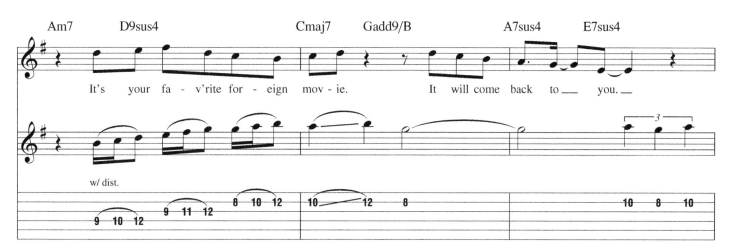

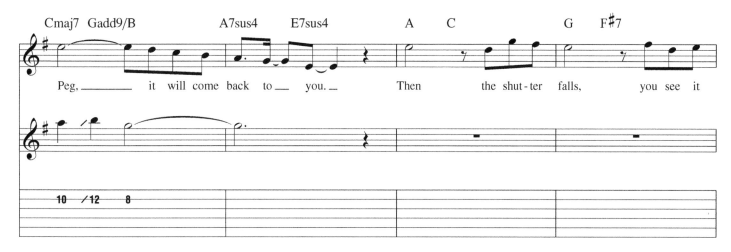

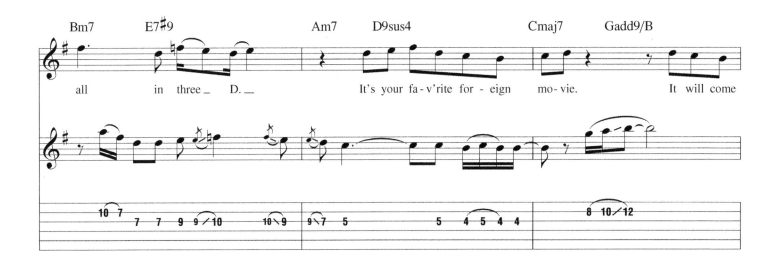

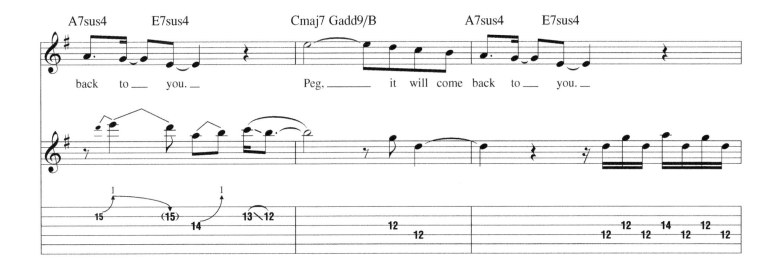

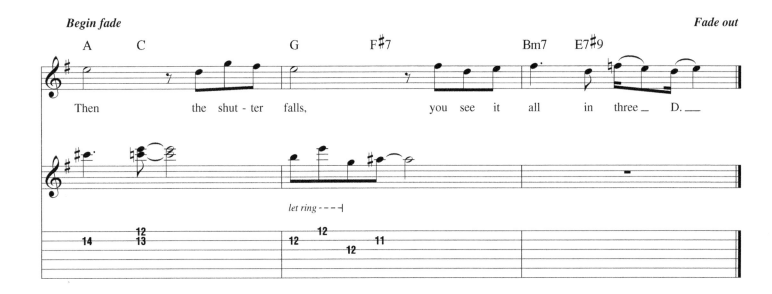

Additional Lyrics

2., 3. I like your pinshot, I keep it with your letter.
Done up in blueprint blue, it sure looks good on you.
And when you smile for the cam'ra, I know I'll love you better.

Pretzel Logic

Words and Music by Walter Becker and Donald Fagen

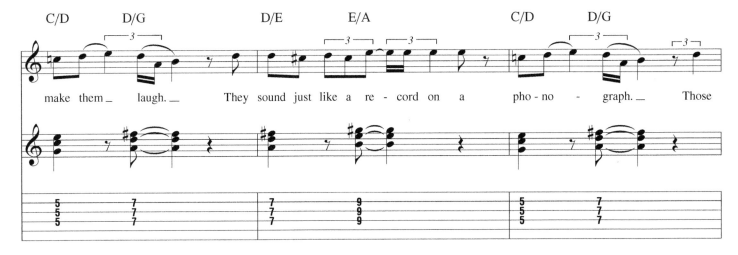

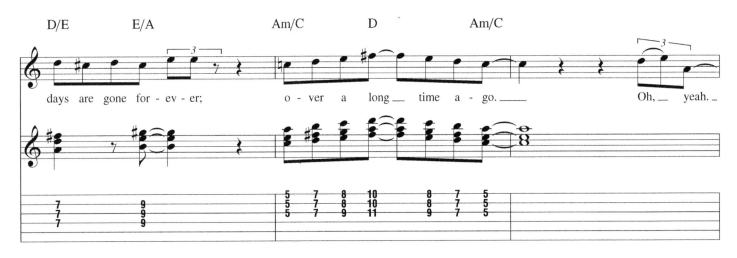

Guitar Solo

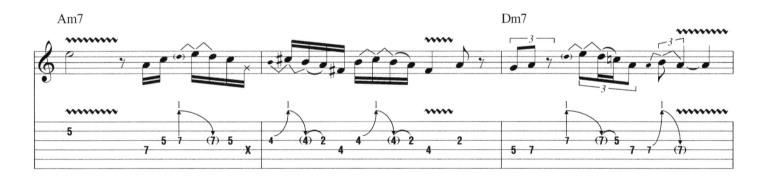

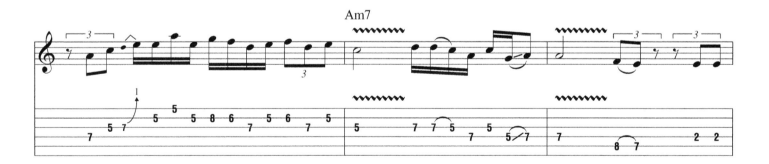

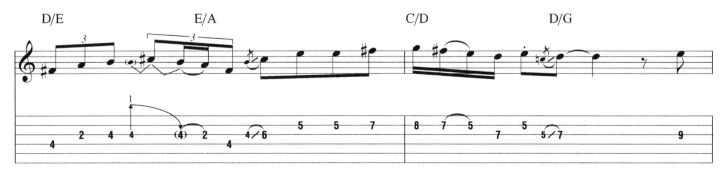

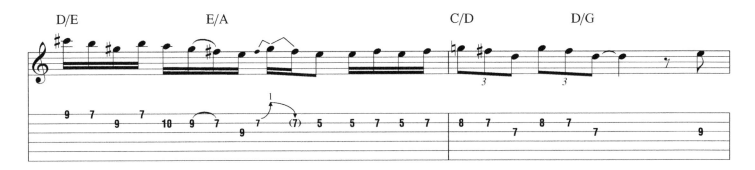

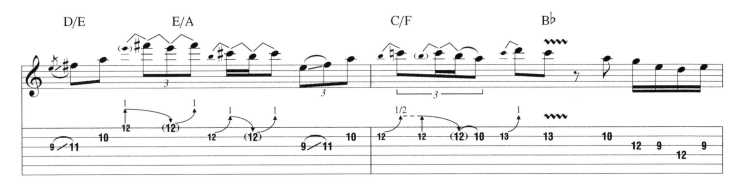

Verse

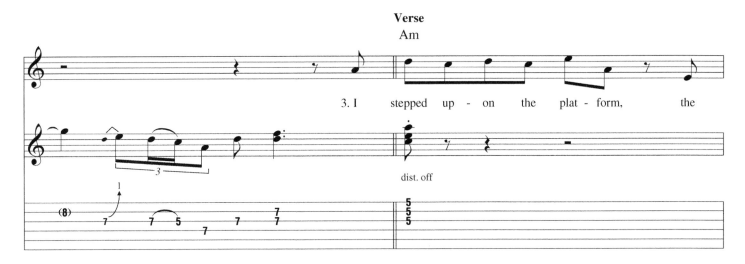

3. I stepped up - on the plat - form, the

dist. off

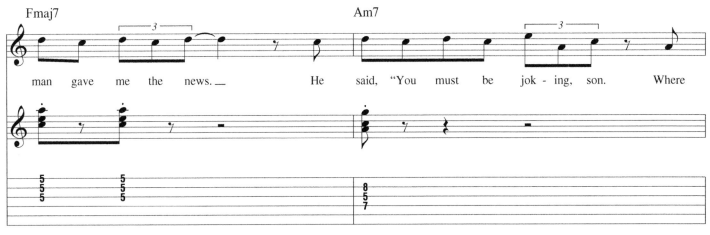

man gave me the news. __ He said, "You must be jok - ing, son. Where

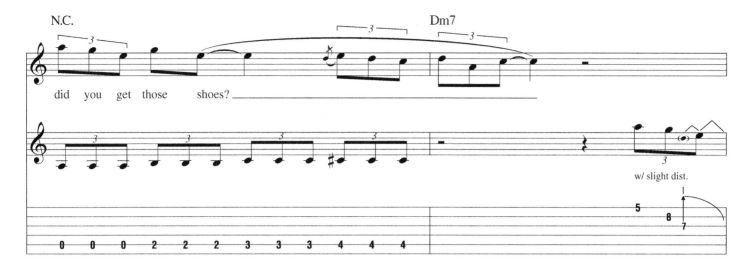

did you get those shoes? _____

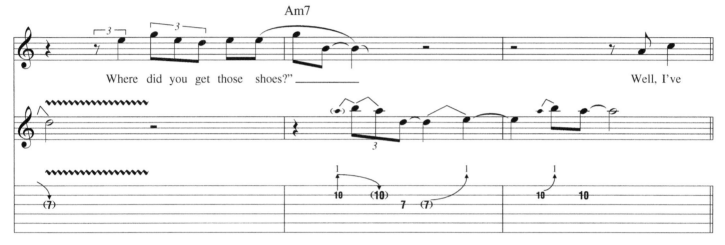

Where did you get those shoes?" _____   Well, I've

Chorus

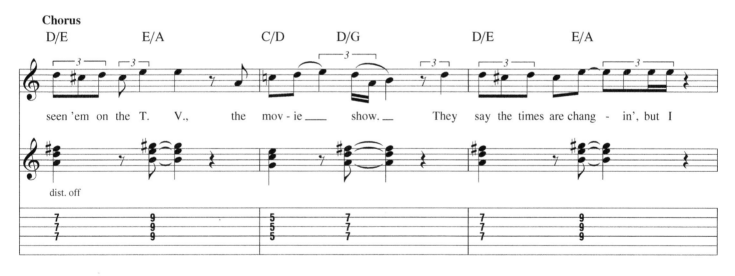

seen 'em on the T. V., the mov-ie ___ show. ___ They say the times are chang - in', but I

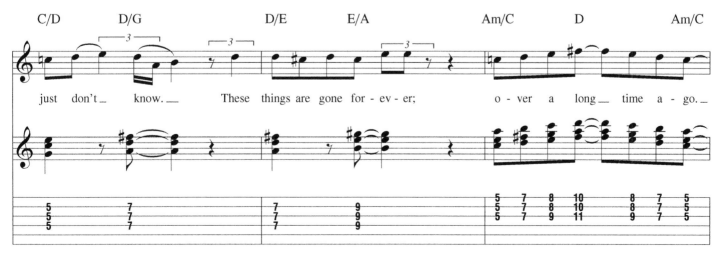

just don't ___ know. ___ These things are gone for - ev - er; o - ver a long ___ time a - go. ___

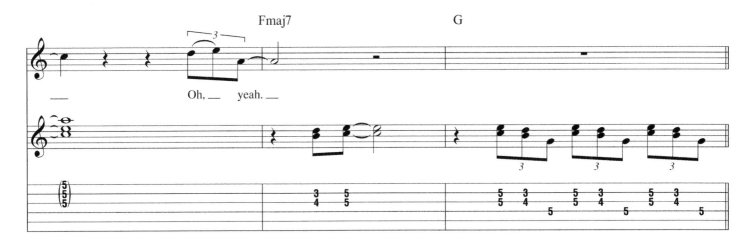

Outro

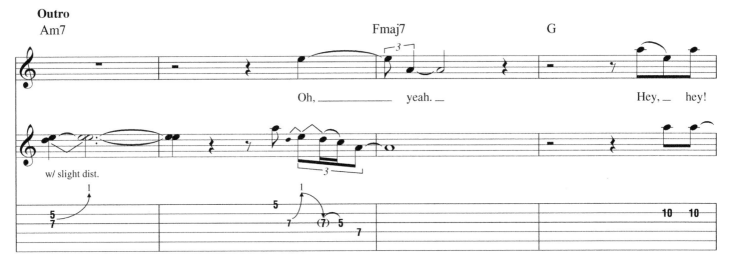

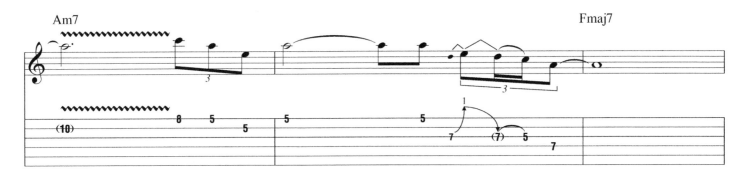

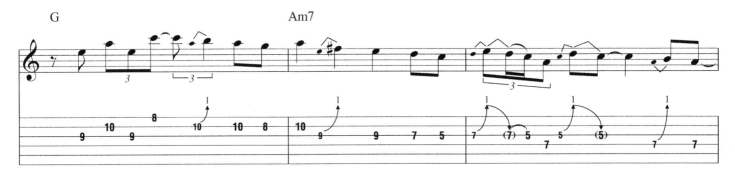

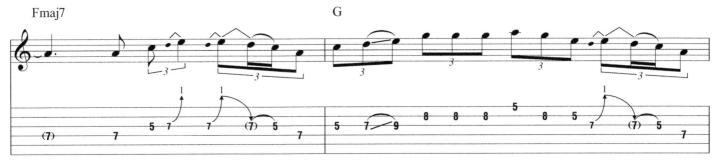

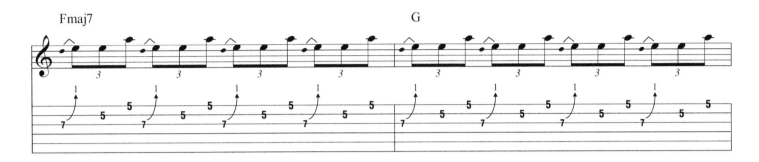

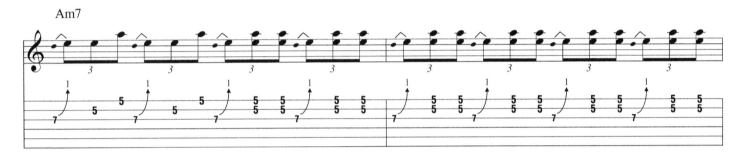

Additional Lyrics

2. I have never met Napoleon, but I plan to find the time.
I have never met Napoleon, but I plan to find the time.
Yes, I do.

Chorus 'Cause he looks so fine upon that hill.
They tell me he was lonely; he's lonely still.
Those days are gone forever; over a long time ago.
Oh, yeah.

Reeling in the Years

Words and Music by Walter Becker and Donald Fagen

Intro
Moderate Rock ♩ = 138

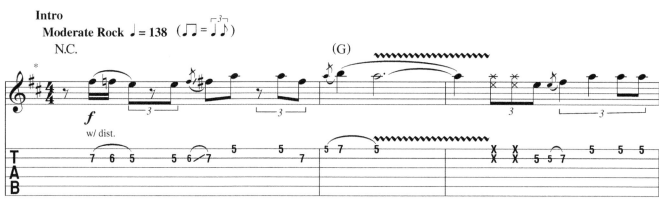

*Key signature denotes A Mixolydian.

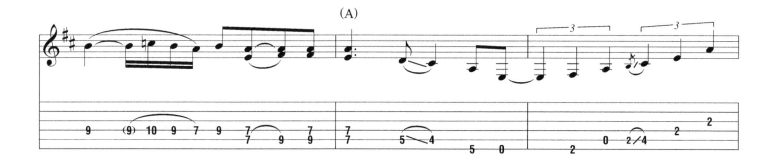

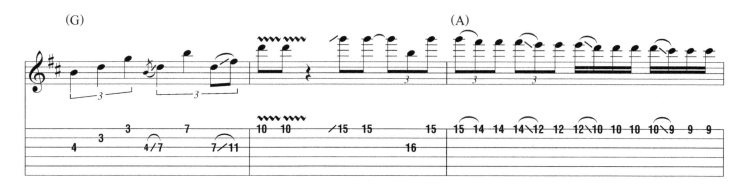

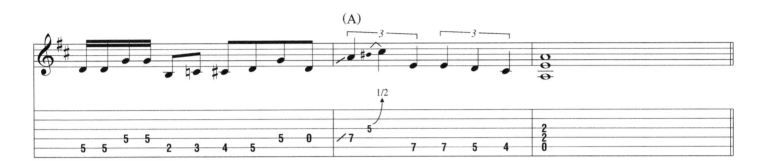

Verse

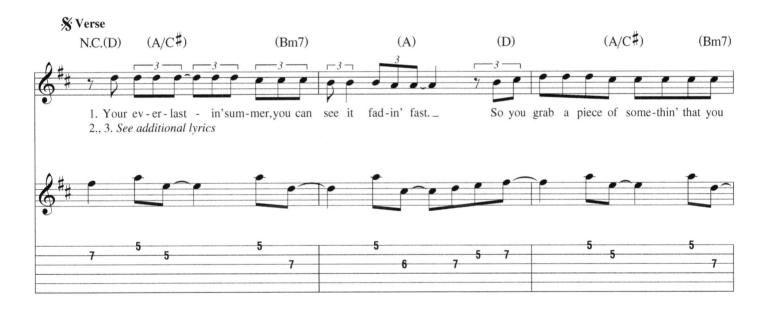

1. Your ev-er-last-in'sum-mer, you can see it fad-in' fast. __ So you grab a piece of some-thin' that you
2., 3. *See additional lyrics*

think is gon-na last. __ Well, you would - n't e-ven know a dia-mond if you held it in your hand. The

tears? ___ Have you had e-nough of mine? _____

Coda 1

Chorus

years; ___ stow-in' a-way the time? ___

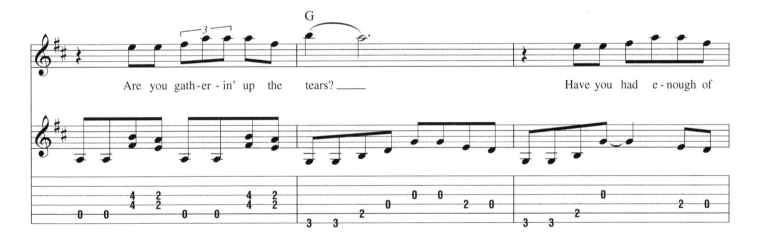

Are you gath-er-in' up the tears? ___ Have you had e-nough of

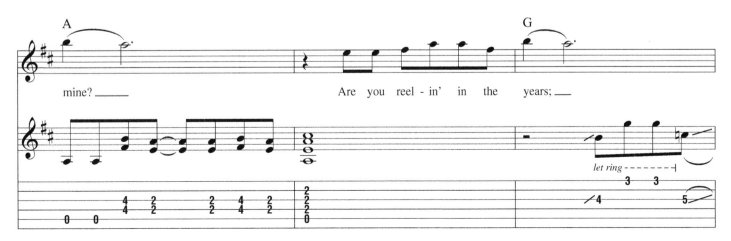

mine? ___ Are you reel-in' in the years; ___

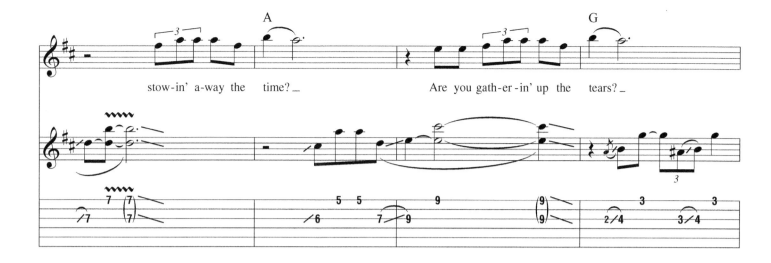

stow-in' a-way the   time? _   Are you gath-er-in' up the   tears? _

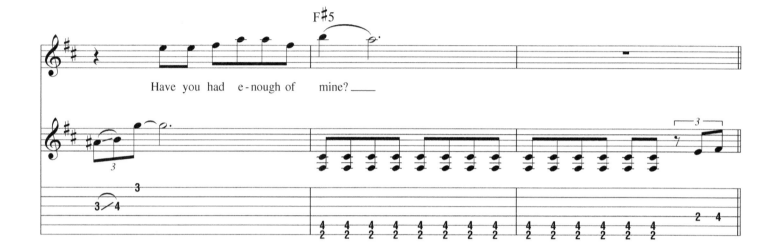

Have you had e-nough of   mine? _____

Interlude

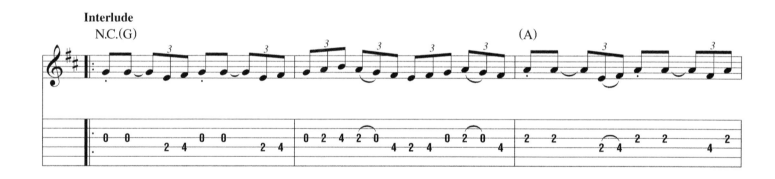

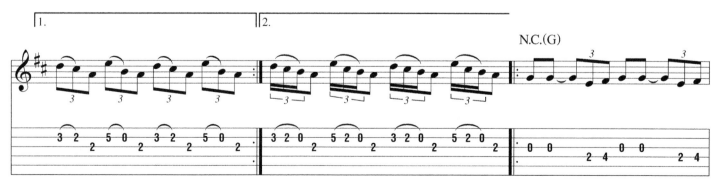

Guitar Solo

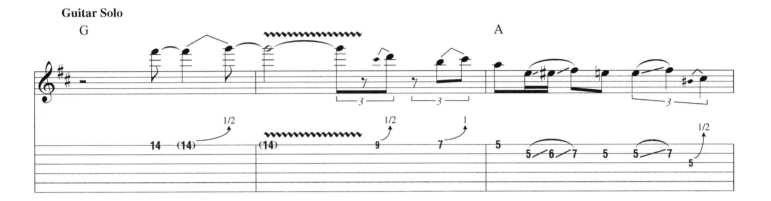

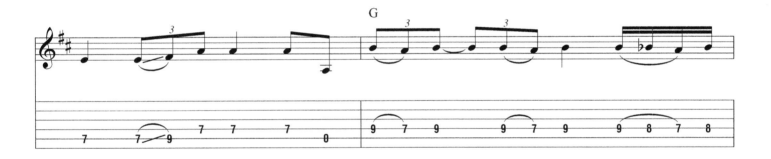

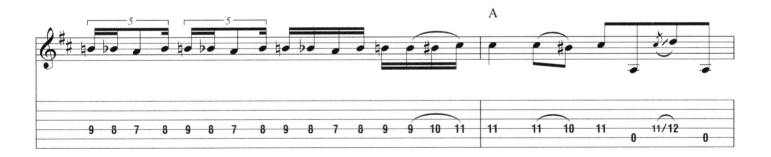

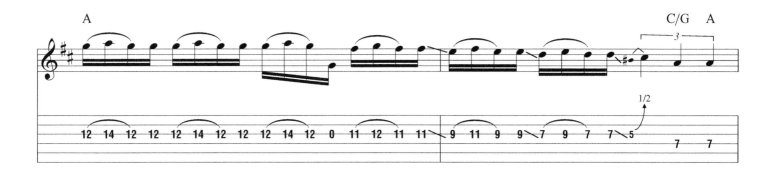

D.S. al Coda 2

⊕ Coda 2

Chorus

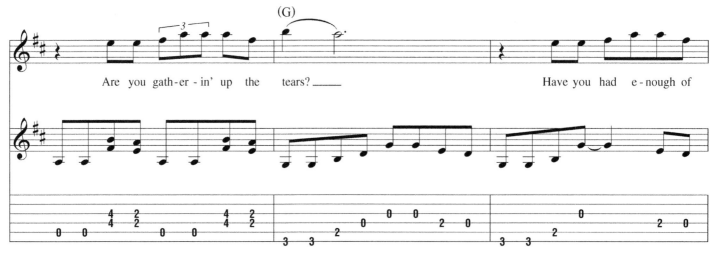

years; _____ stow-in' a-way the time? _____

Are you gath-er-in' up the tears? _____ Have you had e-nough of

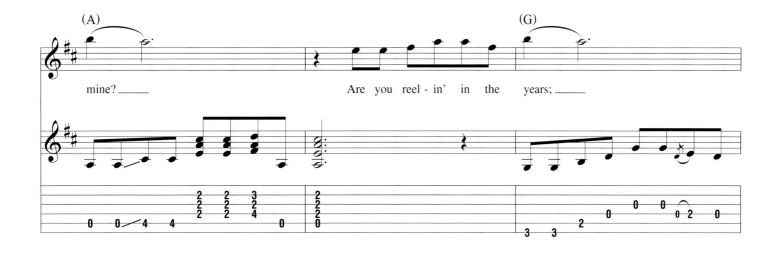

mine? _____   Are you reel-in' in the years; _____

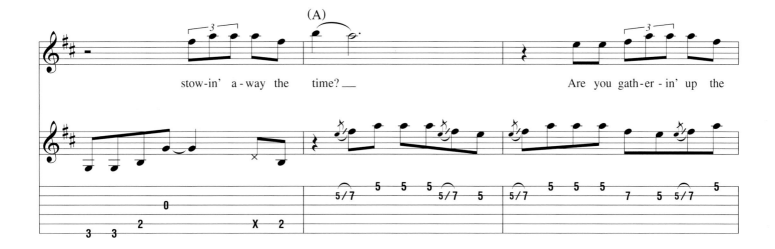

stow-in' a-way the time? ___   Are you gath-er-in' up the

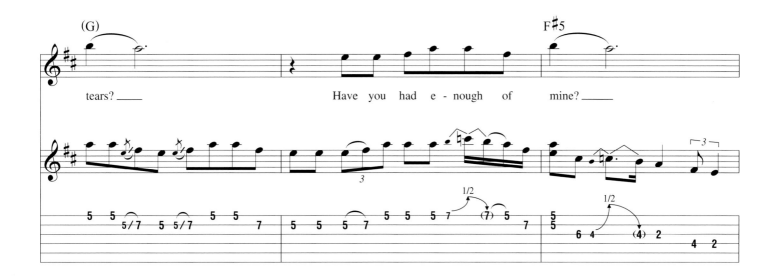

tears? _____   Have you had e-nough of mine? _____

Interlude

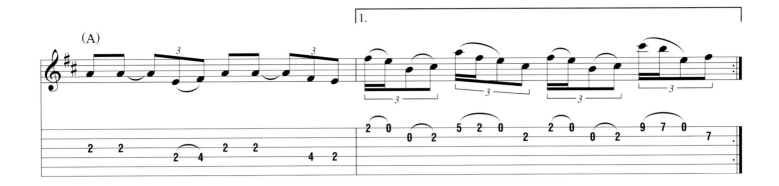

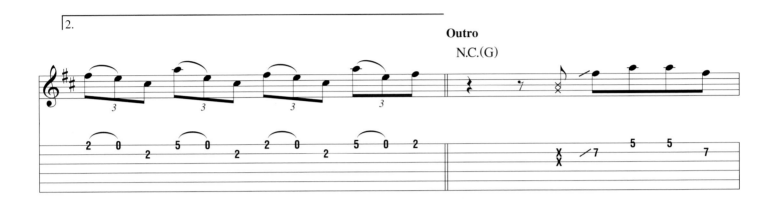

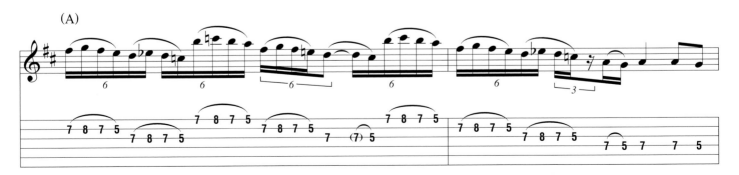

Begin fade

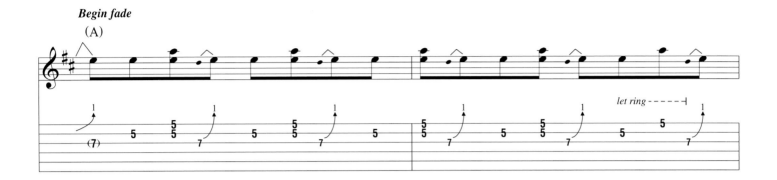

Fade out

Additional Lyrics

2. You've been tellin' me you're a genius since you were seventeen.
   In all the time I've known you I still don't know what you mean.
   The weekend at the college didn't turn out like you planned.
   The things that pass for knowledge I can't understand.

3. I've spent a lot of money and I've spent a lot of time.
   The trip we made to Hollywood is etched upon my mind.
   After all the things we've done and seen you find another man.
   The things you think are useless I can't understand.

HAL•LEONARD GUITAR PLAY-ALONG

Complete song lists available online.

This series will help you play your favorite songs quickly and easily. Just follow the tab and listen to the audio to the hear how the guitar should sound, and then play along using the separate backing tracks. Audio files also include software to slow down the tempo without changing pitch. The melody and lyrics are included in the book so that you can sing or simply follow along.

INCLUDES TAB

VOL. 1 – ROCK ....00699570 / $17.99	VOL. 73 – BLUESY ROCK ....00699829 / $17.99	VOL. 139 – GARY MOORE ....00702370 / $17.99
VOL. 2 – ACOUSTIC ....00699569 / $16.99	VOL. 74 – SIMPLE STRUMMING SONGS..00151706 / $19.99	VOL. 140 – MORE STEVIE RAY VAUGHAN .00702396 / $19.99
VOL. 3 – HARD ROCK ....00699573 / $17.99	VOL. 75 – TOM PETTY ....00699882 / $19.99	VOL. 141 – ACOUSTIC HITS ....00702401 / $16.99
VOL. 4 – POP/ROCK ....00699571 / $16.99	VOL. 76 – COUNTRY HITS ....00699884 / $16.99	VOL. 142 – GEORGE HARRISON ....00237697 / $17.99
VOL. 5 – THREE CHORD SONGS ....00300985 / $16.99	VOL. 77 – BLUEGRASS ....00699910 / $17.99	VOL. 143 – SLASH ....00702425 / $19.99
VOL. 6 – '90S ROCK ....00298615 / $16.99	VOL. 78 – NIRVANA ....00700132 / $17.99	VOL. 144 – DJANGO REINHARDT ....00702531 / $17.99
VOL. 7 – BLUES ....00699575 / $19.99	VOL. 79 – NEIL YOUNG ....00700133 / $24.99	VOL. 145 – DEF LEPPARD ....00702532 / $19.99
VOL. 8 – ROCK ....00699585 / $16.99	VOL. 81 – ROCK ANTHOLOGY ....00700176 / $22.99	VOL. 146 – ROBERT JOHNSON ....00702533 / $16.99
VOL. 9 – EASY ACOUSTIC SONGS ....00151708 / $16.99	VOL. 82 – EASY ROCK SONGS ....00700177 / $17.99	VOL. 147 – SIMON & GARFUNKEL ....14041591 / $17.99
VOL. 10 – ACOUSTIC ....00699586 / $16.95	VOL. 84 – STEELY DAN ....00700200 / $19.99	VOL. 148 – BOB DYLAN ....14041592 / $17.99
VOL. 11 – EARLY ROCK ....00699579 / $15.99	VOL. 85 – THE POLICE ....00700269 / $16.99	VOL. 149 – AC/DC HITS ....14041593 / $19.99
VOL. 12 – ROCK POP ....00291724 / $16.99	VOL. 86 – BOSTON ....00700465 / $19.99	VOL. 150 – ZAKK WYLDE ....02501717 / $19.99
VOL. 14 – BLUES ROCK ....00699582 / $16.99	VOL. 87 – ACOUSTIC WOMEN ....00700763 / $14.99	VOL. 151 – J.S. BACH ....02501730 / $16.99
VOL. 15 – R&B ....00699583 / $17.99	VOL. 88 – GRUNGE ....00700467 / $16.99	VOL. 152 – JOE BONAMASSA ....02501751 / $24.99
VOL. 16 – JAZZ ....00699584 / $16.99	VOL. 89 – REGGAE ....00700468 / $15.99	VOL. 153 – RED HOT CHILI PEPPERS....00702990 / $22.99
VOL. 17 – COUNTRY ....00699588 / $17.99	VOL. 90 – CLASSICAL POP ....00700469 / $14.99	VOL. 155 – ERIC CLAPTON UNPLUGGED.00703085 / $17.99
VOL. 18 – ACOUSTIC ROCK ....00699577 / $15.95	VOL. 91 – BLUES INSTRUMENTALS ......00700505 / $19.99	VOL. 156 – SLAYER ....00703770 / $19.99
VOL. 20 – ROCKABILLY ....00699580 / $17.99	VOL. 92 – EARLY ROCK	VOL. 157 – FLEETWOOD MAC ....00101382 / $17.99
VOL. 21 – SANTANA ....00174525 / $17.99	INSTRUMENTALS ....00700506 / $17.99	VOL. 159 – WES MONTGOMERY ....00102593 / $22.99
VOL. 22 – CHRISTMAS ....00699600 / $15.99	VOL. 93 – ROCK INSTRUMENTALS ....00700507 / $17.99	VOL. 160 – T-BONE WALKER ....00102641 / $17.99
VOL. 23 – SURF ....00699635 / $17.99	VOL. 94 – SLOW BLUES ....00700508 / $16.99	VOL. 161 – THE EAGLES ACOUSTIC ....00102659 / $19.99
VOL. 24 – ERIC CLAPTON ....00699649 / $19.99	VOL. 95 – BLUES CLASSICS ....00700509 / $15.99	VOL. 162 – THE EAGLES HITS ....00102667 / $17.99
VOL. 25 – THE BEATLES ....00198265 / $19.99	VOL. 96 – BEST COUNTRY HITS ....00211615 / $16.99	VOL. 163 – PANTERA ....00103036 / $19.99
VOL. 26 – ELVIS PRESLEY ....00699643 / $16.99	VOL. 97 – CHRISTMAS CLASSICS ....00236542 / $14.99	VOL. 164 – VAN HALEN: 1986-1995 .....00110270 / $19.99
VOL. 27 – DAVID LEE ROTH ....00699645 / $16.95	VOL. 99 – ZZ TOP ....00700762 / $16.99	VOL. 165 – GREEN DAY ....00210343 / $17.99
VOL. 28 – GREG KOCH ....00699646 / $19.99	VOL. 100 – B.B. KING ....00700466 / $16.99	VOL. 166 – MODERN BLUES ....00700764 / $16.99
VOL. 29 – BOB SEGER ....00699647 / $16.99	VOL. 101 – SONGS FOR BEGINNERS .....00701917 / $14.99	VOL. 167 – DREAM THEATER ....00111938 / $24.99
VOL. 30 – KISS ....00699644 / $17.99	VOL. 102 – CLASSIC PUNK ....00700769 / $14.99	VOL. 168 – KISS ....00113421 / $17.99
VOL. 32 – THE OFFSPRING ....00699653 / $14.95	VOL. 104 – DUANE ALLMAN ....00700846 / $22.99	VOL. 169 – TAYLOR SWIFT ....00115982 / $16.99
VOL. 33 – ACOUSTIC CLASSICS ....00699656 / $19.99	VOL. 105 – LATIN ....00700939 / $16.99	VOL. 170 – THREE DAYS GRACE ....00117337 / $16.99
VOL. 34 – CLASSIC ROCK ....00699658 / $17.99	VOL. 106 – WEEZER ....00700958 / $17.99	VOL. 171 – JAMES BROWN ....00117420 / $16.99
VOL. 35 – HAIR METAL ....00699660 / $17.99	VOL. 107 – CREAM ....00701069 / $17.99	VOL. 172 – THE DOOBIE BROTHERS ....00119670 / $17.99
VOL. 36 – SOUTHERN ROCK ....00699661 / $19.99	VOL. 108 – THE WHO ....00701053 / $17.99	VOL. 173 – TRANS-SIBERIAN
VOL. 37 – ACOUSTIC UNPLUGGED ....00699662 / $22.99	VOL. 109 – STEVE MILLER ....00701054 / $19.99	ORCHESTRA ....00119907 / $19.99
VOL. 38 – BLUES ....00699663 / $17.99	VOL. 110 – SLIDE GUITAR HITS ....00701055 / $17.99	VOL. 174 – SCORPIONS......................00122119 / $19.99
VOL. 39 – '80s METAL ....00699664 / $17.99	VOL. 111 – JOHN MELLENCAMP ....00701056 / $14.99	VOL. 175 – MICHAEL SCHENKER ....00122127 / $17.99
VOL. 40 – INCUBUS ....00699668 / $17.95	VOL. 112 – QUEEN ....00701052 / $16.99	VOL. 176 – BLUES BREAKERS WITH JOHN
VOL. 41 – ERIC CLAPTON ....00699669 / $17.99	VOL. 113 – JIM CROCE ....00701058 / $19.99	MAYALL & ERIC CLAPTON.......00122132 / $19.99
VOL. 42 – COVER BAND HITS ....00211597 / $16.99	VOL. 114 – BON JOVI ....00701060 / $17.99	VOL. 177 – ALBERT KING ....00123271 / $17.99
VOL. 43 – LYNYRD SKYNYRD ....00699681 / $22.99	VOL. 115 – JOHNNY CASH ....00701070 / $17.99	VOL. 178 – JASON MRAZ ....00124165 / $17.99
VOL. 44 – JAZZ GREATS ....00699689 / $16.99	VOL. 116 – THE VENTURES ....00701124 / $17.99	VOL. 179 – RAMONES ....00127073 / $16.99
VOL. 45 – TV THEMES ....00699718 / $14.95	VOL. 117 – BRAD PAISLEY ....00701224 / $16.99	VOL. 180 – BRUNO MARS ....00129706 / $16.99
VOL. 46 – MAINSTREAM ROCK ....00699722 / $16.95	VOL. 118 – ERIC JOHNSON ....00701353 / $17.99	VOL. 181 – JACK JOHNSON ....00129854 / $16.99
VOL. 47 – JIMI HENDRIX SMASH HITS....00699723 / $19.99	VOL. 119 – AC/DC CLASSICS ....00701356 / $19.99	VOL. 182 – SOUNDGARDEN ....00138161 / $17.99
VOL. 48 – AEROSMITH CLASSICS............00699724 / $17.99	VOL. 120 – PROGRESSIVE ROCK...........00701457 / $14.99	VOL. 183 – BUDDY GUY ....00138240 / $17.99
VOL. 49 – STEVIE RAY VAUGHAN ....00699725 / $17.99	VOL. 121 – U2 ....00701508 / $17.99	VOL. 184 – KENNY WAYNE SHEPHERD...00138258 / $17.99
VOL. 50 – VAN HALEN: 1978-1984........00110269 / $19.99	VOL. 122 – CROSBY, STILLS & NASH .....00701610 / $16.99	VOL. 185 – JOE SATRIANI ....00139457 / $19.99
VOL. 51 – ALTERNATIVE '90s ....00699727 / $14.99	VOL. 123 – LENNON & McCARTNEY	VOL. 186 – GRATEFUL DEAD................00139459 / $17.99
VOL. 52 – FUNK ....00699728 / $15.99	ACOUSTIC ....00701614 / $16.99	VOL. 187 – JOHN DENVER ....00140839 / $19.99
VOL. 53 – DISCO ....00699729 / $14.99	VOL. 124 – SMOOTH JAZZ ....00200664 / $16.99	VOL. 188 – MÖTLEY CRÜE ....00141145 / $19.99
VOL. 54 – HEAVY METAL ....00699730 / $17.99	VOL. 125 – JEFF BECK ....00701687 / $19.99	VOL. 189 – JOHN MAYER ....00144350 / $19.99
VOL. 55 – POP METAL ....00699731 / $14.95	VOL. 126 – BOB MARLEY ....00701701 / $17.99	VOL. 190 – DEEP PURPLE ....00146152 / $19.99
VOL. 57 – GUNS 'N' ROSES ....00159922 / $19.99	VOL. 127 – 1970s ROCK ....00701739 / $17.99	VOL. 191 – PINK FLOYD CLASSICS ....00146164 / $17.99
VOL. 58 – BLINK 182..........................00699772 / $17.99	VOL. 128 – 1960s ROCK ....00701740 / $14.99	VOL. 192 – JUDAS PRIEST ....00151352 / $19.99
VOL. 59 – CHET ATKINS ....00702347 / $17.99	VOL. 129 – MEGADETH ....00701741 / $17.99	VOL. 193 – STEVE VAI ....00156028 / $19.99
VOL. 60 – 3 DOORS DOWN ....00699774 / $14.95	VOL. 130 – IRON MAIDEN ....00701742 / $17.99	VOL. 194 – PEARL JAM ....00157925 / $17.99
VOL. 62 – CHRISTMAS CAROLS.............00699798 / $12.95	VOL. 131 – 1990s ROCK ....00701743 / $14.99	VOL. 195 – METALLICA: 1983-1988 ......00234291 / $22.99
VOL. 63 – CREEDENCE CLEARWATER	VOL. 132 – COUNTRY ROCK ....00701757 / $15.99	VOL. 196 – METALLICA: 1991-2016 ......00234292 / $19.99
REVIVAL ....00699802 / $17.99	VOL. 133 – TAYLOR SWIFT ....00701894 / $16.99	
VOL. 64 – ULTIMATE OZZY OSBOURNE....00699803 / $19.99	VOL. 135 – MINOR BLUES ....00151350 / $17.99	*Prices, contents, and availability subject to change without notice.*
VOL. 66 – THE ROLLING STONES...........00699807 / $19.99	VOL. 136 – GUITAR THEMES ....00701922 / $14.99	
VOL. 67 – BLACK SABBATH...................00699808 / $17.99	VOL. 137 – IRISH TUNES ....00701966 / $15.99	
VOL. 68 – PINK FLOYD –	VOL. 138 – BLUEGRASS CLASSICS.........00701967 / $17.99	
DARK SIDE OF THE MOON ....00699809 / $17.99		
VOL. 71 – CHRISTIAN ROCK ....00699824 / $14.95		

www.halleonard.com

0222
173